danceclub

tango

danceclub
tango

paul bottomer

southwater

For Elaine, my wife and partner,
to whom I owe my deepest debt of love, respect and gratitude

This edition is published by Southwater

Southwater is an imprint of Anness Publishing Ltd
Hermes House, 88–89 Blackfriars Road, London SE1 8HA
tel. 020 7401 2077; fax 020 7633 9499
info@anness.com

Published in the USA by Southwater,
Anness Publishing Inc.
fax 212 807 6813

This edition distributed in the UK by
The Manning Partnership
tel. 01225 852 727; fax 01225 852 852

This edition distributed in the USA
by National Book Network
tel. 301 459 3366; fax 301 459 1705

This edition distributed in Canada by
General Publishing
tel. 416 445 3333; fax 416 445 5991

This edition distributed in Australia by
Pan Macmillan Australia
tel. 1300 135 113; fax 1300 135 103

This edition distributed in New Zealand by
The Five Mile Press (NZ) Ltd
tel. (09) 444 4144; fax (09) 444 4518

A CIP catalogue record for this book is available from the British Library.
Publisher: Joanna Lorenz
Senior Editor: Lindsay Porter
Photographer: Anthony Pickhaver
Make-up: Karen Fundell
Designer: Siân Keogh

Previously published as *Dance Crazy Tango Argentino*

1 3 5 7 9 10 8 6 4 2

Contents

Introduction

Passionate, sensual and tantalizing, the Tango is many things to many people. In the European and International styles, there are many dances from which to suit the mood of the moment – the romance of the Waltz, the ebullience of Rock 'n' Roll, or the carnival atmosphere of Samba. Despite its reputation as a melancholic dance, Tango captures all these moods and more. Born of life's experience in the back street gutters of Buenos Aires, the Tango rose from its humble beginnings to dazzle at high class Parisian soirées, yet the back street bars remained its true home among the people who had given it life.

In the closing years of the nineteenth century, Europe had been ravaged by wars, famine and economic uncertainty. With few prospects and little hope of a stable life in the land of their birth, many young men emigrated to begin a new life in South America. Many hundreds of thousands disembarked in the new federal capital of Argentina, the port of Buenos Aires on the Rio de la Plata.

Despite a high degree of prosperity in Argentina at this time, life was hard for the immigrants, being forced to live in the squalid outskirts of the city. Despite this, the immigrants kept coming, and by 1914 outnumbered native-born Argentinians in Buenos Aires by three to one. About half of the immigrants were Italian, and about a third Spanish. The old port area of Buenos Aires, la Boca, where many Italians settled, is a colourful reminder of the Italian contribution to the history of Tango.

By the advent of the immigrants, the life of the famous Argentinian cowboys, known as "gauchos", had all but disappeared, so the romantic image we have of Rudolph Valentino dancing a rather theatrical version of the Tango in the 1924 film, *The Four Horsemen of the Apocalypse,* is erroneous. However, in the days when gauchos did roam the prairies, news was carried by *payadores,* who were a type of travelling minstrel, improvising songs on current themes. From these songs came a style of song, and later a dance called the Milonga. The records for this period are vague, but we know that the Milonga enjoyed great popularity in Buenos Aires, particularly among the poorer classes.

The emergence of the word "Tango" is shrouded in mystery, but the word is thought be African in origin, and denotes a "meeting place" or "special place". This does not mean the Tango itself is of African origin. The Cuban Habanera,

Right: The Tango originated in the back street cafés of Buenos Aires.

the Spanish Contradanza and the Afro-Argentinian Candombé all influenced the evolution of the Tango, but no dance more than the Milonga. Milonga itself means "party" or "fiesta" and the music itself was lively, vivacious and joyful. What evidence there is suggests that *compadritos* frequently visited Afro-Argentinian dances and then may have borrowed some of the moves and adapted them to the Milonga, paving the way for the Tango-Milonga variant.

The new Argentinians of European descent shared a common bond, but one that often found currency in despair and disillusionment. This poured out into song, the song of sadness, nostalgia and longings, but also of hope and aspiration. The passion of the song demanded further expression in a dance, and so it was that in the back street gutters of Buenos Aires, the Tango was born.

The vast majority of the immigrants to Argentina were young men, who eventually outnumbered women by fifty to one. These young men were often frequent visitors to the *academias* (from "dance academy") and *pregundines,* low-life cafés where the waitresses could be hired for dancing. In order to attract the women, it became very important for the young men to become good dancers. The Tango not only acquired the taste of forbidden fruits in these cafés, but the men who could dance it well, and who therefore had their choice of women, acquired a very macho image. With no real dance academies, men would teach each other the Tango, exchange steps and practise together before exercising their skills to attract the women. Freed from the conventions of European dances, the men would devise very practical and often unique ways of skilfully leading the women. Some of these will be explored later as we uncover some of the secrets of dancing Tango. Women, too, would dance together, to lure the men.

The first instruments to accompany the Tango were the guitar, flute and violin. Eventually, though, the bandoneon became the crucial instrument. It is often remarked that the bandoneon is the soul of the Tango, and Tangos have been written which pay homage to that "instrument of the devil". The bandoneon was originally the invention of a German, Heinrich Band (hence bandoneon), who designed the instrument as a substitute for the church organ in parishes too poor to afford the real thing. It is a sort of squeeze-box concertina with keys at both ends, and notoriously difficult to play. The legend of the Tango has many strange twists, and it is said that the bandoneon first came to Argentina when a Swedish freighter, the *Landskrona* arrived in Buenos Aires in 1868. A seaman, having parted with his last peso, was forced to exchange his bandoneon for a final bottle of Schnapps.

With the exception of some vocal Tangos, most feature the bandoneon. "La Cumparsita", perhaps the best known Tango in the world, dates from 1916, and was composed originally as a march by Gerardo Matos Rodriguez. Later adapted as a Tango, "La Cumparsita" means a small street band or

Right: The bandoneon, the instrument which has come to symbolize the soul of Tango.

procession in a carnival. Another very famous Tango composed in 1905 by Angelo Villoldo is "El Choclo". This has endured as one of the most popular Tangos of all time, and, in the 1950s, had a new lease of life when the release of a new arrangement, "Kiss of Fire", launched it into the American popular charts, creating a testament to the timelessness of Tango.

With the deep, sonorous and breathy notes of the bandoneon, the Tango became more earthy, intense and brooding, and even sometimes, but not always, melancholy. Words were added to the melodies, which reflected the preoccupations of the people. The principal themes evoked by the Tango lyricists adopted a fatalistic view and focused on the trials of life as they saw them. Carlos Gardel became the greatest Tango singer of all time. Gardel was the archetypal Latin lover, and was tragically killed in an air crash in 1935. His grave in the cemetary of La Chacarita in Buenos Aires has since

Below: The old port area of Buenos Aires, known as La Boca, is a colourful reminder of the Italian contribution to the development of Tango.

become a place of pilgrimage. Many of Gardel's vocal Tangos had only a guitar accompaniment, reflecting the style of the old *payadores.* The first Tango to be performed by Gardel was "Mi Noche Triste" ("My Sad Night") in 1917. The sentiments are typical of Tango lyrics, and express the sorrow of an abandoned lover consoling himself with drink.

Enrique Santos Discepolo, one of the foremost Tango poets and composers, said "Tango is a sad thought expressed in dance". To me, however, Tango is not so much a thought as an impulse that challenges the dancers to explore their inner feelings through dance.

The Universal Suffrage Law 1912 gave a new freedom to the people, and an impetus to the Tango. Now, it was not only the lower classes who wanted to dance the Tango, but it also became fashionable for high society to throw Tango parties, and Tango salons were quickly established in the upper-class areas of Buenos Aires. The fame of Tango soon spread from South America to New York, London and Paris, where Tango tea-dances became the rage.

However, the uncompromising and daring character of the Tango placed it in immediate conflict with authority figures. In Paris, Cardinal Amette declared "Christians should not in good conscience take part in it" and the following year, Pope Benedict XV complained "It is outrageous that this indecent, heathen dance, which is an assassination of family and social life, is even being danced in the Papal residence". In 1914, Kaiser Wilhelm II forbad his officers to dance the Tango while in uniform, describing the dance as "lascivious, and an affront to common decency".

As the First World War raged on, people sought distractions from its horror and, despite the turmoil of the time, the Tango was far from forgotten. The mood of the time was changing, and there was a new sense of freedom in the air. The adventure of the Tango reflected that mood, and the demand for it continued to grow. Dance schools, salons and ballrooms boomed with Tango classes and dances. As the war came to an end, Tango entered its golden age of the 1920s. As it became more and more popular in Europe and North America, in Buenos Aires its popularity had reached unprecedented heights. While the masses adored the Tango, some musicians strived to interpret it in new and innovative ways as a musical art form. These musicians and composers were greatly admired, and became household names in Buenos Aires and beyond. Bandoneon players became almost like gods. But it was not only the musicians who captured the imagination – the great dancers, too, were adulated by the people. Perhaps the best known and most enduring reputation was held by the legendary El Cachafaz (José Ovidio Bianquet). Dancing with Carmencita Calderon, El Cachafaz was revered by the public. The greatest Tango dancers of recent times must be Juan Carlos Copes and Marie Nieves. They are the embodiment of the dance, and never fail to inspire and touch those who witness their Tango.

Left: The woman dances the sensuous Ocho.

In more recent times, there have been many Tango dancers made famous by their appearance in spectacular shows around the world. Their style, however, is Show Tango, and over the years, it has grown less and less to resemble the authentic Tango of Buenos Aires. This is in no way to diminish the skill, expertise and sheer quality of the performance, but this book is about how two ordinary people can come together to dance the Tango.

A military coup on 6 September 1930 in Argentina heralded a period of unsettled government, during which the authorities, nervous and anxious to control any possible criticism, started to ban any Tango which had any political innuendo, or sang of social injustice.

In Europe, the Tango had undergone a massive evolution. The Argentine Tango, while popular, did not accord with the long-held European ideas about dancing, and the authentic style was quickly and ruthlessly changed. Walks were introduced to make the dance progress around the ballroom floor, and the seductive character of the Tango was suppressed beneath a faster, harsher, more aggressive beat. Drums, which were hardly used in the Argentinian *Orquestra Typica,* added to the staccato, march-like quality of this "modern" Tango, and encouraged a sharper interpretation, including the highly stylized head jerks

associated with the modern international style of competitive Tango. The couple no longer looked at each other, and the smouldering passion of the authentic Argentine Tango had been dragged from its mysterious and seductive intimacy to be paraded around the dance floor in a style more ostentatious than intimate.

During the 1950s in Buenos Aires, the Tango went into decline. Peron fell from power, and the health of the economy moved precariously downwards. The immigrants no longer viewed themselves as immigrants, but as Argentinians, and the power of the Tango to console nostalic longing had waned. With ecomonic decline, there were less funds to promote the huge Tango events and orchestras typical of the 1940s. Tango was still played by smaller groups, but now the audience listened rather than danced. By the 1960s, musicians and composers were experimenting with "el nuevo Tango", a new style of Tango music for listening to. As this grew in popularity, so the interest in Tango as a dance declined. However, some notable orchestras and composers, including the celebrated Osvaldo Pugliese, continued to play for enthusiastic audiences both in Argentina and abroad. During the 1980s, large-scale productions also went on tour around the world, stimulating a revival of interest outside Argentina. Such was their effect, that a new generation discovered Tango for the first time, and came under its spell. Now, Tango clubs, salons and schools are once again springing up throughout North America, Europe and the Far East.

The Tango has come a long way from its humble beginnings, but it has a long way to go yet. Its history is inextricably tangled with legend, romantic exaggeration and nostalgic reminiscence, and is all the richer for it. Tango is a sensual dance, which captures the full gamut of human emotion, of hope, disappointment and life itself. *Esto es Tango* - This is Tango !

Left: Today, Argentine Tango retains the intimacy of the original dance.

Tango Tongue Twisters	
El Retroceso – retro-ssessoe	**Los Tres Ochos** – tress o-choss
La Salida – sall-edda	**La Trabada** – tra-ba-da
La Cunita – kun-eeta	**La Parada** – pa-ra-da
La Resolucion – reso-loo-see-on	**La Llevada** – zhay-va-da
El Ocho – 0-cho	**La Sentada** – sen-ta-da
El Ocho Abierto – o-cho abbey-air-toe	**Los Ochos Largos** – o-chos lar-ghos
La Ronda – ron-da	**La Media Luna** – may-deeya loona
El Pepito – pép-ee-toe	

What to Wear

What to wear will depend largely on the salon you are visiting. At a *milonga* in Buenos Aires, dress will be fairly casual. Outside Argentina, while there are not usually specific dress codes, there are often unspoken conventions. During one visit to a Tango salon in Amsterdam, a newcomer arrived in a dress with a bright floral design, which contrasted markedly with the predominantly black apparel of the other *tangueros*. Black has a number of romantic associations with the Tango. Since Tango is a dance of the midnight hour and of the shadows, it is often thought that black is appropriate. Many early photographs of Tango dancers show them in black or dark colours. In fact, this was largely due to the fact that, in the early years of this century, cheap chemical dyes were only just becoming available and black clothes were the most inexpensive and practical for workwear. Hats are not normally worn these days, except for shows, when the almost obligatory grey or black fedora completes the man's outfit.

Women's dress is more variable. Younger women tend to select "tube" dresses or something fitted. Older women may choose a split skirt or dress to allow freedom of movement. Sleeveless designs which are plain and without frills are appropriate to the Tango. With regard to colour, if in doubt, wear black.

a fedora may be worn for exhibition Tango

women's dresses will be fitted, but will allow for movement

women's shoes will have a heel

men's shoes may be patent leather

Getting Started

If you have danced any other Tango before, it would be as well not to transfer any of the characteristics of that dance to the Tango Argentino, as this is a very different dance. It does not have the angry staccato interpretation of the modern international-style Tango, but is smoother and much more sensuous and seductive. This Tango is to be danced by two people for each other rather than to be performed. The dance is more important than the dancers and, if this is respected, the dance will repay the dancers' respect a thousandfold.

During the course of the book, we will be introducing and working through some of the basic popular moves of the Tango Argentino. Each element is fully explained. By following the instructions exactly, you will find that

Left and right: Tango Argentino is a much more intimate style of dance than modern Tango, and is well suited to dancing in small settings.

the moves are not difficult and, with practice, you will soon be dancing Tango in the authentic style of Buenos Aires.

Figures or moves are explained step by step and then joined together with other figures to build up a complete group of figures. These groups can then be repeated or followed by any of the other groups of figures in the book. As you learn one group and progress to the next, you will find that the elements of the next group are already familiar to you. It is particularly important therefore to ensure that you are happy and comfortable with each element before moving on. In this structured way, you will quickly increase both your vocabulary of moves and your pleasure in dancing them.

The most important aspect of any dancing is to enjoy what you are doing at whatever level. While technical excellence can yield enormous pleasure, it is equally possible to find pleasure in learning to Tango with each new step. Now relax and try the first group.

Group One

El Retroceso – La Salida – La Cunita – La Resolucion

The first group of figures combines some of the basic moves in Tango Argentino. Once this basic group has been mastered, you will be able to dance, practise and enjoy Tango continuously. While dancing Group One, you will make approximately a quarter turn (or 90°) to the left.

EL RETROCESO (THE REVERSE START)

The opening movement of the Tango is called the Salida. However, the Salida incorporates many varied starting elements, so the opening move is separated here from the rest of the Salida for the sake of clarity. The Retroceso, or the Reverse Start, is one of the most easily led, practical and popular starts. The man and woman start with their feet together. The man is standing on his left foot and the woman corresponds by standing on her right foot.

1 Man
Walk backwards with the right foot, taking a short step. (Count – slow)
Woman
Walk forward with the left foot. (Count – slow)

2 Man
Step to the side with the left foot, taking a wider step than the woman. (Count – slow)
Woman
Step to the side with the right foot, taking a shorter step than the man. (Count – slow)

La Salida (The Continuation of the Start)

For the man it is very important not to turn in Step 1 of the Salida. Turning can be avoided by ensuring that the woman does not take too wide a side step during the Retroceso. In Step 2, the man squeezes the woman between his hands, leading her to move away from him and creating a space into which the woman can cross her feet on Step 3.

1 Man

Walk forward with the right foot between yourself and the woman. Ensure there is no turn.
(Count – slow)

Woman

Walk backwards with the left foot.
(Count – slow)

2 Man

Walk forward with the left foot, turning the body slightly to the right. (Count – quick)

Woman

Walk backwards with the right foot, taking a slightly longer step and turning slightly to the right to ensure the shoulders remain parallel with the man's.
(Count – quick)

3 Man

Close the right foot to the left foot and end standing on the right foot. (Count – quick)

Woman

Cross the left foot in front of the right foot – this need not be a tight cross. End standing on the left foot.
(Count – quick)

Style Tip

For the woman in Step 2, the backwards step with the right foot should be large enough to allow an easy cross on the next step. In Step 3, the woman may feel she is turning away from the man. This serves to maintain her disinterested stance. The knees should be together, but not necessarily the feet. The cross in Step 3 is called a "trabada", which means "fastened".

LA CUNITA (THE CRADLE)

This simple figure comprises a step followed by a crossing tap, producing a gentle rocking motion which gives the step its name. This figure is particularly useful because it can be repeated, allowing the couple to avoid others and to manoeuvre into a clear space on a crowded floor. From the end of the Salida, the couple gently rotate anticlockwise on the first step of the Cunita, so that this figure is danced almost side by side. There is then no danger of treading on your partner's feet.

▼1 Man
Walk forward with the left foot. (Count – slow)
Woman
Walk backwards with the right foot.
(Count – slow)

▼3 Man
Walk backwards with the right foot.
(Count – slow)
Woman
Walk forward with the left foot. (Count – slow)

▲2 Man
Standing on the left foot, tap the right foot across and behind the left foot. (Count – &)
Woman
Standing on the right foot, tap the left foot across the right foot.
(Count – &)

▲4 Man
Standing on the right foot, tap the left foot across the right foot.
(Count – &)
Woman
Standing on the left foot, tap the right foot across and behind the left foot. (Count – &)

LA RESOLUCION (THE CLOSING FINISH)

In this movement, the man and woman "resolve" the previous moves in a conclusion which once again brings them together. This movement is also sometimes called "El Cierre". This group, like many of the best Tangos, should be allowed to resolve itself gently, as in a caress, and under no circumstances should the feet be stamped or closed strongly. While there is a variety of movements which can be used to end a figure, this one is the most common and most practical, as it leaves the dancers standing on the appropriate foot, ready to start the next group with the Retroceso.

1 Man

Walk forward with the left foot, starting to turn to the left. (Count – quick)

Woman

Walk backwards with the right foot, starting to turn to the left. (Count – quick)

DanceTip

In Step 3, the foot is "peeled", heel first, from the floor and then placed gently, heel last, to close with straight legs On slow counts, the ball of the foot usually touches the floor first.

2 Man

Step to the side with the right foot, continuing the turn. (Count – quick)

Woman

Step to the side with the left foot, continuing the turn. (Count – quick)

3 Man

Close the right foot
to the left foot.
(Count – slow)

Woman

Close the right foot
to the left foot.
(Count – slow)

Style Tips

Once the pattern, steps and timing have become familiar, you can start to improve the look and feel of your Tango by enhancing the style. This, however, takes some practice. Remember that Tango evolved naturally and, while many movements may be stylized, the feeling is smooth and effortless. The best Tango is understated.

When dancing a forward or backwards walk or a side step to a slow count of music, it considerably enhances the style if the body is held quite still while the foot is placed in position. When this has been done, the feet should remain still while the body moves from one foot to the other. This gives the Tango moves their characteristic feline quality and inner strength. It is said that the essence of Tango is stillness and that "less is more".

On slow counts, even on forward walks, the ball of the foot usually touches the floor first. This has been described like dancing as if on broken glass. The result is that the dance has a very purposeful and considered look, which is a feature of Tango danced by an expert.

As a general rule, when the feet close tightly, the legs will straighten on the preceding step and remain straightened for the close or tight cross. A good example of this occurs in Steps 2 and 3 of the Salida and Steps 2 and 3 of the Resolucion.

It is undesirable to move too vigorously or to take large steps. Smaller steps, which are clear and accurate, are preferable and have much more feeling.

Group Two

El Retroceso – La Salida – El Ocho – La Resolucion

I n the second group, the Cunita is replaced by one of the most popular figures in Tango, the Ocho. "Ocho" is simply the Spanish word for "eight" and the figure is so-called because the woman seductively describes a figure of eight on the floor in front of the man. In Tango, there are many figures in which the movement alternates from the man to the woman and vice versa. The Ocho is one such figure, where the members of the couple are not dancing the opposite of their partner's steps. First dance the Retroceso and the Salida. The man now has his feet closed and is standing on the right foot. The woman has crossed the left foot in front of the right foot and is standing on the left foot.

EL OCHO (THE EIGHT)

1 Woman
Release the right foot and lift the lower right leg parallel to the floor, ensuring that the knees remain firmly together. Move the right foot to the right, causing the body to rotate anticlockwise as you swivel on the left foot. (Count – &)

2 Woman
Still with the knees together, point the right foot forward between yourself and the man and outside the man's right side.
(Count – slow)

3 Woman

Transfer your weight forward to stand on the right foot, knees still together. Standing on the right foot, lift the left foot so that the lower left leg is parallel to the floor. Move the left leg to the left, causing the body to rotate clockwise as you swivel on the right foot. (Count – &)

4 Woman

Still with the knees together, point the left foot forward between yourself and the man. (Count – slow)

5 Woman

Transfer your weight forward to stand on the left foot, knees still together. Lift the right foot just clear of the floor and swivel on the left foot to face the man. (Count – &)

The Man's Movements

While the woman dances the Ocho, the man can remain in position with the feet closed, relaxing the knees slightly to await the completion of the woman's move. Alternatively he can join in the movement, in which case the figure becomes the Doble Ocho.

EL DOBLE OCHO (THE DOUBLE EIGHT)

In this figure, the woman's steps remain the same. When the man feels the woman turning at the beginning of the Ocho, he joins her.

1 Man

With the feet still closed, swivel on the right foot to maintain the shoulders parallel to the woman's. (Count – &)

> ### MUSIC SUGGESTION
>
> "Delusion" by Orchestra Tango Café (Sounds Sensational) is an excellent Tango with a clear beat and a steady tempo ideal for the first-time dancer.

2 Man

Point the left foot backward, matching the woman's right foot and leg. (Count – slow)

3 Man

Complete the transfer of your weight back onto the left foot and straighten the leg in preparation for a close. (Count – &)

4 Man

Close the right foot to the left foot, legs straight. (Count – slow)

5 Man

Hold the position while guiding the woman to face you. (Count – &)

Style Tip

During this and similar maneuvers, the man must not use his arms to turn the woman. Rather, his arms must maintain a firm frame in relation to his body. If he feels he must use his arms, he should turn the whole body and frame.

During the Ocho, the woman should either look in the direction in which she is moving or maintain eye contact with the man. The man should look at the woman throughout, or he could suggest that he is leading the woman by casting his gaze first to the right and then to the left in anticipation of the woman's steps. This is a neat and effective tip which will appear later on.

Conclude Group Two with the Resolucion. Now try dancing Groups One and Two alternately following each other. If danced correctly, you will be dancing along the four sides of a square.

Leading

A lot of nonsense is often talked about leading. Leading, contrary to the popular image, is not a case of the man making the woman dance a particular figure or move. Rather, a good lead from the man merely makes clear his intention to the woman, who then follows. The Tango dancer Juan Carlos Copes once remarked about leading, "The man should always remember that he is dancing with a lady." This is sound advice.

KEEPING PARALLEL SHOULDERS

The first ingredient of a good lead is for the man to dance his own moves clearly and confidently. Clarity from the man is all-important, as it enables the woman to detect the speed, direction and feel of a figure early enough to respond appropriately.

The woman will generally be aware of where and how the man is moving by following the alignment of his shoulders and trying to maintain a parallel position between her shoulders and his. Try dancing Groups One, Two and Three slowly without holding your partner, using only the maintenance of parallel shoulders as a guide.

Left: The woman follows the alignment of the man's shoulders as a lead.

A STEADY FRAMEWORK

Right: The upper body and arms of the man provide a "frame" with which to lead the woman.

The man's arms and upper body make a firm frame in which the woman is gently held. The man must not allow his arms to move independently of his upper body, as this destroys the frame. He must never be seen to "steer" the woman with his arms. Leads are a subtle but clear communication between the dancers and should not be visible to others.

The woman should not try to anticipate the man's intentions but should wait to accept and follow the man's lead.

In some specific figures, the man will squeeze the woman firmly between his hands to produce, for example, a turn as in the Parada. Specific leads such as these are dealt with in the section on that particular figure.

As we explore Tango Argentino, there is always something new and unexpected. Uniquely in Tango, some leads may be given with the foot or leg. This concept is explored further in the section dealing with Sacadas.

Orientation

It is important, especially in the early stages of learning to Tango, that you try to adhere to the given orientation or "alignment" of the figures, as distortions look as well as feel awkward. In Step 2 of the Retroceso, the man steps to the side with no turn. The position of his left foot now determines the line of travel of the remainder of the group.

Group Three

El Retroceso – Modified Salida – El Ocho Abierto – La Resolucion

Having had some practice at dancing the Ocho, you can now try a more expressive version, the Ocho Abierto, or the "open eight."

Begin this group with the Retroceso, then dance a modified Salida. Note the change of timing as the Salida is modified.

MODIFIED SALIDA

▼ 1 Man

Walk forward with the right foot between yourself and the woman. (Count – quick)

Woman

Walk backward with the left foot. (Count – quick)

▲ 2 Man

Walk forward with the left foot but turn your body one-eighth of a turn to the right. (Count – quick)

Woman

Walk backward with the right foot keeping parallel shoulders with the man. (Count – quick)

▼ 3 Man

Hold the position with the right foot behind. Flex the left knee and swivel to the left on the left foot, maintaining parallel shoulders with the woman. Do not extend either arm, as the woman goes on to dance the Ocho. (Count – slow)

Woman

Walk forward with the left foot, crossing past the right foot onto the man's line. (Count – slow)

EL OCHO ABIERTO (THE OPEN EIGHT)

◀ 1 Man

Hold the position. Swivel on the left foot to maintain parallel shoulders. (Count – &)

2 Man

Hold the position. Swivel on the left foot to maintain parallel shoulders. (Count – slow)

1–5 Woman

Dance an Ocho in front of the man. (Counts – &, slow, &, slow, &)

◀ 3 Man

Hold the position. Straighten the left leg. (Count – &)

▶ 5 Man

Hold the position, while guiding the woman to face you. (Count – &)

◀ 4 Man

Close the right foot to the left foot with straight legs. (Count – slow)

Conclude Group Three with the Resolucion. To help clarify exactly when the man closes, it is helpful to count the man's steps, starting at the beginning of the group. The group has ten steps and the man will close on Step 7.

Styles of Tango

While it is sometimes said that there are as many styles of Tango as there are bars in Buenos Aires, in reality there are only three predominant styles.

SHOW TANGO

Perhaps the style most widely seen by the general public is show Tango, which is the breathtaking version seen in the series of Broadway and West End Tango productions of recent years. This is a stylized stage variant and it is the remaining two styles which are the most commonly seen in Buenos Aires and in the many Tango clubs, schools, salons and *milongas* around the world. These come under the broad heading of the "Tango de salon" and it is in this style that the real magic of Tango can be found.

THE LINEAR TANGO

In this style, the movements are built up moving along a line such as those in Groups One, Two and Three. It can also be danced, by not turning the Resolucion, to track anticlockwise around a medium to large floor such as a ballroom. This is a slightly more formal style of Tango than the rotary style.

THE ROTARY TANGO

This is a style more suited to smaller floors such as those of Tango cafés and bars. In this type of Tango, the man and woman weave intricate figures around each other while taking up very little space. This style is definitely more intimate.

Group Four

El Retroceso con la Ronda – La Revolucion –
El Doble Ocho – La Resolucion – Los Tres Ochos

The next new figure to be introduced is the Revolucion, which requires very little space and in which the man and woman move around each other in intimate exploration. As before, the group also includes some moves with which you are already familiar.

EL RETROCESO CON LA RONDA (THE REVERSE START WITH THE CIRCLE)

1 Man
Walk backward with the right foot with the knee flexed, leaving the left foot in place. (Count – slow)

1, 2 Woman
Dance the Retroceso as usual. (Counts – slow, slow)

2 Man
Circle the left foot counterclockwise to close to the right foot, without transferring your weight onto the left foot. As this is part of a continuing movement, the knees remain flexed.
(Count – slow)

LA REVOLUCION (THE FULL TURN)

1 Man

Extend the left foot forward past the woman's left side and point it at the woman's back foot.
(Count – slow)

Woman

Extend the left foot forward past the man's left side and point it at the man's back foot.
(Count – slow)

2 Man

Transfer your weight forward onto the left foot, swivelling to face the woman and closing the right foot to the left foot, legs straight. End standing on the right foot. (Count – slow)

Woman

Transfer your weight forward onto the left foot, swivelling to face the man and closing the right foot to the left foot, legs straight, without transferring your weight onto the right foot. End standing on the left foot.
(Count – slow)

Style Tip

I t is not necessary and not good style to power the turn in Step 2.

Summary of the Turn

El Retroceso con la Ronda – no turn

La Revolucion – half turn (or 180°) anticlockwise

El Doble Ocho – quarter turn (or 90°) anticlockwise

La Resolucion – quarter turn (or 90°) anticlockwise

By the end of the group, you will have made one complete turn.

Continue to turn a further quarter turn anticlockwise, and complete the group by dancing the Doble Ocho and the Resolucion described earlier.

Los Tres Ochos (Three Eights)

This figure comprises three Doble Ochos. Dance the Retroceso con la Ronda and the Revolucion.

▼ **1** Man
Continue to make a further quarter turn (or 90°) anticlockwise by swivelling to the left on the right foot. (Count – &)

▼ **3** Man
Transfer your weight back onto the left foot. (Count – &)

▲ **2** Man
With your shoulders parallel to the woman's, point the left foot straight back, keeping your weight on the right foot. (Count – slow)

4 Man

Close the right foot
to the left foot.
Straighten the legs
and end standing on
the right foot.
(Count – slow)

5 Man

Hold the position,
guiding the woman
to face you.
(Count – &)

Repeat moves 1–4
twice more, curving
very gently to the
left. No more than a
half turn should be
made by the man
during this figure.

Style Tip

The man should ensure that he uses
his right forearm to keep the woman
dancing the Ochos in front of him and
not under his right arm.

The Woman's Movements

Dance three Doble Ochos as normal,
but turning a little more on the left foot
to match the man. Make the forward
steps with the right foot a little shorter
and the forward steps with the left foot
a little longer, to finish facing the man
at the conclusion of each Ocho.

*Complete this variation of Group
Four with the Resolucion.*

Group Five

El Retroceso – El Pepito – La Trabada – La Resolucion

The Pepito is named after the Tango master Pepito Avellaneda of Buenos Aires, who uses this figure extensively. This is a delightful and witty basic construction and one which you will later be able to develop into an introduction to many interesting variations and combinations.

Start by dancing the first two steps of the Retroceso. The man is now standing on the left foot with the feet apart. The woman is standing on the right foot with the feet apart, having taken a shorter side step than the man.

EL PEPITO

3 Man
Close the right foot to the left foot but remain standing on the left foot.
(Count – slow)
Woman
Cross the left foot behind the right foot, using only the ball of the foot.
(Count – slow)

4 Man
Move the right foot diagonally forward.
(Count – slow)
Woman
Swivel a one-eighth turn to the right on the left foot and move back onto the right foot.
(Count – slow)

Style Tip

In Step 4, the line between the man's feet and the line between the woman's feet should be parallel.

32

4 & Man

Close the left foot to the right foot but remain standing on the right foot. You can tap the left foot if you like. (Count – &)
Walk forward with the left foot outside the line of the woman's right foot. (Count – slow)

Woman

Swivel a one-eighth turn to the left on the right foot, allowing the left foot to close but keeping your weight on the right foot. (Count – &)
Walk backwards with the left foot. (Count – slow)

5 Man

Walk forward with the right foot in line with the woman's right foot.
(Count – slow)
Woman
Walk backwards with the right foot, taking a slightly longer step and turning slightly to the right in preparation for the Trabada.
(Count – quick)

5 & Man

Hold the position, allowing the woman to cross in her Trabada.
(Count – &)
Woman
Trabada: cross the left foot in front of the right foot. End on the left foot.
(Count – quick)

> *Continue with the Resolucion or dance the Cunita or the Doble Cunita and Doble Ocho before concluding with the Resolucion.*

Cortes

We have already touched on the drama of the Tango as the dancers explore their relationship through the dance. Each in turn may take the lead and many moves can be improvised, although improvisations must maintain the character of the Tango. It is during these improvisations that a conflict of intention may arise. In these circumstances, the dance may come to a sudden halt while the conflict is resolved. Such a halt, though not a figure in itself, is called a "Corte." To an onlooker, this often serves to heighten the suspense before the drama moves on. In reality, the man must now indicate and clarify his intentions to the woman. There are many ways of doing this within the character of the dance and many elaborate devices have been invented over the years.

THE SHOESHINE

Let us suppose that the couple has danced the Retroceso, when suddenly the man feels that the woman is in doubt as to which foot she is to use in the next move. The couple stop – a *Corte*. The man now indicates to the woman which foot he has free and, in so doing, he shows her which foot she must use next. In the Shoeshine, the man remains on his left foot with the knee slightly flexed and rubs his right foot slowly up and down the calf of his left leg, as if polishing his shoe. There is no timing for this gesture. Suffice it to say that the couple resume the dance in time with the music.

La Puntada del Pie (The Foot Tap) — La Levantada

In a similar gesture to the Shoeshine, the free foot can be tapped repeatedly against the floor. The Puntada may also be performed by the woman while the man is dancing the Shoeshine, just to show her irritation at being kept waiting!

A very useful corte for the woman is the Levantada. When the couple comes to a standstill with the feet apart, the woman may perform a Levantada by lifting the free foot so that the knees are together and the lower leg is parallel with the floor. She then gently swings the free foot from side to side in an expectant gesture.

AMAGUE

A different type of embellishment is an Amague, where a threatening gesture is made. An Amague is also sometimes danced to express frustration or to warn of a following figure which may be fast, sharp and dramatic. A stamp or harsh tap called a "frappé" executed immediately before the next dramatic movement is a good example of an Amague. While less experienced dancers may enjoy interspersing their dancing with a peppering of Amagues, the effect is lost if the following figure does not live up to its dramatic announcement. Good Tango dancers therefore use this type of embellishment sparingly and only in the proper context of announcing the severe or powerful nature of the following move.

MUSIC SUGGESTION

"El Amancer" by Carlos di Sarli (MH/Sicamericana Corp.) Meaning "the dawn," legend has it that the composer, Roberto Firpo, was inspired to write this magical Tango while walking home after performing at an all night party. Listen to the violins as they recreate the dawn chorus.

Group Six

El Retroceso – El Americano – El Doble Ocho – La Resolucion

In Group Six, you will again encounter familiar components, as well as learn a new and exciting move called the Americano. Because this figure moves to the side, it is particularly useful to dance if the way ahead is blocked by other dancers or the perimeter of the floor.

Start by dancing the Retroceso, but this time the man leads the woman to take a step as wide as his own on Step 2. This is done simply by transmitting a gentle pressure through the right forearm.

EL AMERICANO (THE AMERICAN)

The man leads into the Americano by gently but firmly pressing downwards with his right hand, suggesting to his partner that she will not be moving backwards as she might otherwise expect. He can then induce his partner to complete the figure by "playing" her between his hands within the toned framework of his arms.

1 Man

Tap the right foot across and behind the left foot, with the knees together and no turn. End with the right foot at knee height.
(Count – slow)

Woman

Tap the left foot across and behind the right foot, with the knees together and no turn. End with the left foot at knee height.
(Count – slow)

2 Man

With the knees tightly together, move the right foot to the right, the lower leg parallel with the floor, and swivel to the left on the left foot. (Count – &)

Woman

With the knees tightly together, move the left foot to the left, the lower leg parallel with the floor and swivel to the right on the right foot. (Count – &)

3 Man

Walk forward and across with the right foot between yourself and the woman. End standing on the right foot. (Count – slow)

Woman

Walk forward and across with the left foot between yourself and the man. (Count – slow) Swivel to the left on the left foot to face the man. (Count – &)

Conclude the group with the Doble Ocho and the Resolucion.

Group Seven

El Retroceso – La Parada – El Sandwich –
El Ocho – La Resolucion – La Llevada

Another classic Tango figure is introduced here. The Parada is a super figure, allowing even inexperienced dancers to feel the magic of Tango in the Rotary style. Again, this group starts with the Retroceso. The man has ended standing on his left foot and the woman on her right. To dance the next figure, the woman's right foot should be roughly opposite a point halfway between the man's feet.

LA PARADA (THE STOP)

In this figure, the man "stops" the woman with a combination of his right hand and confirmatory contact of his right foot with her left foot.

1 Man

Hold the position. Lead the woman by squeezing her with your right hand towards your left hand. The hands should be at approximately the same height from the floor, although the left hand is often very slightly higher. Keep the left hand and arm still and firm and do not rotate the body. Apply base of hand pressure with the right hand to turn the woman for the Parada. (Count – slow)

Woman

Facing square to the man, cross the left foot loosely behind the right foot to a point opposite the man's left foot to aid balance. (Count – slow)

2 Man

Leading the woman back across yourself at 90° toward the right, slide the right foot forward in a curve. Keep the foot in contact with the floor but without weight and, with the inside edge of the ball of the right foot, make contact with the outside edge of the ball of the woman's left foot. End with the knees together, left knee flexed and right leg straight. (Count – slow)

Woman

Swivel a quarter turn (or 90°) to the right on the left foot and step backward onto the right foot. Flex the right knee with the left leg held forward, knees together.
(Count – slow)

EL SANDWICH

This figure is also known as "La Mordita" ("the bite"). During the move, the woman's left foot is sandwiched between the man's feet.

1 Man

Transfer your weight forward onto the right foot and close the left foot to the right foot, sandwiching the woman's left foot. End facing the woman with legs straight.
(Count – slow)

Woman

Hold the Parada position. (Count – slow)

2 Man

Swivel a quarter turn (or 90°) to the right on the left foot and step backward onto the right foot. Flex the right knee with the left leg held straight forward, knees together.
(Count – slow)

Woman

Transfer your weight forward onto the left foot. (Count – slow)

EL OCHO (FOLLOWING EL SANDWICH)

1 Man

Move the left side of
the body forward
over the left foot.
(Count – slow)

Woman

Walk forward with
the right foot over
the man's left foot.
Do not turn.
(Count – slow)

2 Man

Swivel a little to the
right on the left foot
to maintain the
relationship with the
woman and to lead
her turn. Keep the
left leg straight.
(Count – &)

Woman

Swivel to the right
on the right foot,
dancing an Ocho.
(Count – &)

3 Man

Close the right foot
to the left foot. End
standing on the right
foot. (Count – slow)

Woman

Point the left foot
forward to a position
in front of the man,
knees together.
Transfer your
weight forward onto
the left foot.
(Count – slow)

4 Man

Hold the position,
while guiding the
woman to face you.
(Count – &)

Woman

Swivel on the left
foot to face the man
with the right foot
held just clear of the
floor. (Count – &)

> *Complete the
> group with the
> Resolucion.*

LA LLEVADA – A CLASSIC FOOT LEAD

Tango is full of many exciting embellishments which are fun to dance and impressive to see. Many look very difficult but are really quite easy once you know how. One embellishment of the Parada is the Llevada. This move is also known as a Barrida (a "sweep") or a Corrida del Pie (a "slide of the foot"). In this example the Llevada is danced between the Parada and the Sandwich.

Man's Tip
After completing the Parada, you will be standing on the left foot, having just contacted the woman's left foot with your right foot. Step 3 of the Llevada is more comfortable if you flex the right knee and lift the right heel clear of the floor while moving the woman's foot. If your standing foot is likely to get in the way of the woman's moving foot, do not step back away from the woman, but create enough space by simply taking a wider step.

Woman's Tip
It is important to offer a little resistance to the man's foot as he slides yours. The effect of many Llevadas has been ruined by the woman's anticipation.

1 Man
Transfer your weight forward onto the right foot, facing the woman. Tap the inside of the woman's left foot lightly with the inside of your left foot. (Count – &)
Woman
Hold the Parada position. (Count – &)

2 Man
Still facing the woman, step to the side with the left foot, around the woman. It is important to remember to step around the circle. (Count – slow)
Woman
Hold the Parada position. (Count – slow)

3 Man

Standing on the left foot with the left knee flexed, use the right foot to slide the woman's left foot around the circle. End with the knees together and with the right foot pointing forward and across, as at the end of the Parada. (Count – slow)

Woman

Offering a little resistance to maintain contact, allow the man to move your left foot while you swivel on your right foot. (Count – slow)

The figure may be repeated up to three times before continuing with the Sandwich.

Cadencia

It is true that in the Tango Argentino the timing of the moves may alter according to the preference of the dancers, the mood or the demands of the music. In this book, the timings given are those which, through experience, have been found to be the most suitable in all circumstances and there is rarely any good reason to alter them. The timings and descriptions given enable newcomers to the Tango to share a common understanding of what to do and how to do it in order to experience success, satisfaction and pleasure in dancing the Tango.

It is, however, good style to start and end moves with the phrasing of the music, or the "cadencia". An experienced *tanguero* is able to achieve this by using skilful combinations of figures, cortes and embellishments.

While Groups One, Two and Three each correspond to four bars of music and will therefore match its phrasing if started at the beginning of a musical phrase, the Parada group lasts five bars. In order to use cadencia, a dancer might therefore follow the Parada group with the Retroceso, the Salida and the Resolucion, which take up three bars of music. The five bars of the Parada group and the three bars of the Retroceso-Salida-Resolucion combination will then equal eight bars and will match the musical phrasing, or cadencia.

Group Eight
El Retroceso – La Sentada – El Ocho – La Resolucion

The Sentada is another popular and classic figure in Tango Argentino. The woman moves to a position on the man's left side which suggests that she is sitting on his knee, hence the name Sentada, or "chair".

Start with the by now familiar Retroceso but, to lead the Sentada, the man takes a slightly wider step and moves the left foot a little forward in Step 3. The left knee flexes, while the right leg remains straight.

LA SENTADA (THE CHAIR)

The lead in the Sentada is different from the lead in the Parada. In the Parada, the couple remains facing in Step 3 and the man squeezes the woman between his hands. In the Sentada, the man rotates his frame, causing the woman to turn.

1 Man

Hold the feet in position. Lead the woman to turn by rotating the frame anticlockwise. (Count – slow)

Woman

Standing on the right foot, swivel a quarter turn (or 90°) to the left. Step back underneath the body with the left foot and relax the left knee. (Count – slow)

▶2 Man

Hold the position. (Count – &)

Woman

Continue turning slightly on the left foot and relax down to contact the man's left knee as if to sit, but without weight. Lift the right foot to contact the outside of your left knee, toes pointing to the floor. (Count – &)

3 Man

Hold the position.
Lead the woman to
turn by rotating the
frame clockwise.
(Count – slow)

Woman

Lower the right foot
to the floor, making
a small forward
step. (Count – slow)

4 Man

Holding the feet in
position, straighten
the left leg.
(Count – &)

4 – 6 Woman

Continue by dancing
an Ocho, ending on
the left foot and
facing the man.
(Counts – &,
 slow, &)

▶ 5 Man

Close the right foot
to the left foot with
legs straight. End
standing on the right
foot. (Count – slow)

6 Man

Hold the position,
while guiding the
woman to face you.
(Count – &)

MUSIC SUGGESTION

"A Media Luz" by Olivia Molina
(Indoamerica). This gentle yet passionate Tango, is captured perfectly
in this excellent vocal version. For a
non-vocal version try Gran Orquestra
Tipica (Orfeon).

Continue with the Resolucion or
the Doble Ocho or Tres Ochos, as
danced following the Revolucion
in Group Four.

Group Nine
El Retroceso – La Salida – Los Ochos Largos – La Resolucion

We have already seen how the Ocho fulfils an important role in the Tango. Let us now explore an easy but interestingly flexible Ocho group in the rotary style.

Start by dancing the standard Retroceso and Salida. The man is now standing on the right foot with feet together. The woman has just danced the Trabada and has therefore crossed the left foot in front of the right foot and is standing on her left foot.

LOS OCHOS LARGOS

In this figure, the woman dances a series of continuous Ochos. Each time she steps forward with the right foot, however, she makes contact with the inside of the man's right foot.

1 Man
Step to the side with the left foot. (Count – slow)

2 Man
Walk forward with the right foot between yourself and the woman. (Count – slow)

3 Man
Swivel to the right on the right foot to face the woman and step to the side with the left foot. (Count – slow)

4 Man

Repeat Step 2.

5 Man

Repeat Step 3.

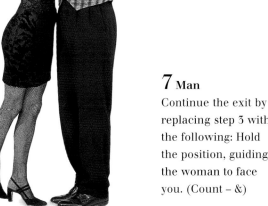

6 Man

To exit from the figure, replace Step 2 with the following: Close the right foot to the left foot. End standing on the right foot. (Count – slow)

7 Man

Continue the exit by replacing step 3 with the following: Hold the position, guiding the woman to face you. (Count – &)

Group Ten
La Media Luna

The Media Luna is a super figure for less experienced *tangueros*, as each step has a "slow" count, giving you plenty of thinking time. The figure also features many of the moves encountered earlier in the book. For more experienced dancers, it is an excellent figure to combine with others. Some of the many options are explained here.

LA MEDIA LUNA (THE HALF MOON)

In this figure, Step 4 for the woman is the Parada, which she learnt in Group Seven.

2 **Man**
Step to the side with the left foot. (Count – slow)
Woman
Step to the side with the right foot. (Count – slow)

1 **Man**
Walk backwards onto the right foot. (Count – slow)
Woman
Walk forward onto the left foot. (Count – slow)

3 Man

Cross the right foot behind the left foot and stand on the right foot with the knees flexed. (Count – slow)

Woman

Facing square to the man, cross the left foot loosely behind the right foot to a point opposite the man's left foot. (Count – slow)

4 Man

Hold the feet in position, while leading the woman to dance a Parada as previously described in the Parada section. (Count – slow)

Woman

Swivel a quarter turn (or 90°) to the right on the left foot and move backwards onto the right foot - this is a Parada. The right knee will be flexed while the left leg is held straight forward, knees together. (Count – slow)

◀**5** Man

With the feet in place, start to untwist to the right, swivelling on both feet. During this movement a quarter turn (or 90°) to the right will be made. (Count – slow)

Woman

Take a wide step to the side with the left foot. (Count – slow)

▶ **6** Man

Still swivelling to the right, make a further quarter turn (or 90°) to the right. The feet will now be completely uncrossed and will end apart. Straighten the left leg in preparation for a close, ending standing on the left foot. (Count – slow)

Woman

Take a good walk forward onto the right foot. (Count – slow). Standing on the right foot, swivel a half turn (or 180°) to the right. (Count – &)

7 Man

Close the right foot
to the left foot with
straight legs.
(Count – slow)

Woman

Point the left foot
forward to a point
opposite the man.
(Count – slow)

8 Man

Hold the feet in
position, guiding the
woman to face you.
(Count – slow)

Woman

Transfer your
weight forward onto
the left foot and
swivel on the left
foot to face the man.
(Count – slow)

Woman's Tip

While the appearance of the Media
Luna suggests that the couple are moving in a half circle, in fact the best way
to dance the figure with clarity is for the
woman to understand that she is really
dancing in a rectangle. The position of
the left foot in Step 3 can be thought of
as the first corner. In Step 4, you will
turn and then step back onto the second
corner. Step 5 will move you to the next
corner and Step 6 to the final corner.

---

*Continue with the Resolucion, the
Double Start or the Basic Start.*

The Double and Basic Starts

In the introduction to the Salida in Group One, we saw how this opening figure can have several starting elements. For simplicity and easy compatibility with the standard Resolucion, so far we have only used the Retroceso (the "reverse start"). Here is an alternative to the Retroceso as an entry to the Salida when danced from the end of the Media Luna.

THE DOUBLE START

1 Man
Step to the side with the left foot, leaving the right foot in place.
(Count – quick)
Woman
Step to the side with the right foot, leaving the left foot in place.
(Count – quick)

2 Man
Transfer your weight sideways onto the right foot, closing the left foot to the right foot but without weight.
(Count – quick)
Woman
Transfer your weight sideways onto the left foot, closing the right foot to the left foot but without weight.
(Count – quick)

THE BASIC START

The Basic Start may be used instead of the Double Start and is simply Step 3 of the Double Start. Within the framework of the figures and groups presented in this book, the Basic Start can only be danced after the Media Luna.

3 Man
Step to the side with the left foot, taking a wider step than the woman's. (Count – slow)
Woman
Step to the side with the right foot, taking a shorter step than the man's. (Count – slow)

Basic and Double Starts Following the Salida or the Ocho

If you particularly enjoy the Basic or Double Start, it is possible to dance either following directly from the end of the Salida or the Ocho. The man and woman must ensure, however, that they become square to each other and that the woman is in a neutral position before the Basic or Double Start, that is to say that she has not already committed herself to the Resolucion.

Continue with the Salida or the Modified Salida.

Combinations

In this section of the book, we look at some of the figures you have already been learning and see how they can be combined, so you can enjoy dancing some very impressive, exciting but nonetheless practical and very danceable moves in the Tango.

COMBINATION ONE – *El Retroceso – La Salida – La Doble Cunita – El Doble Ocho – La Resolucion*

In this easy combination, you can combine some of the first figures you learnt.

1 Dance the Retroceso and the Salida as in Group One.

2 Then dance one Cunita...

3 ...followed by another Cunita.

COMBINATION TWO – *El Pepito – La Parada – La Llevada – El Sandwich*

The fluidity of this combination yields an amazing feeling of rapport between the man and the woman. It looks tricky but then you don't have to tell anyone how easy it really is.

Dance up to Step 5 of the Pepito. After the Parada, continue with either the Llevada or the Sandwich.

1 The Pepito Step 1.

2 The Pepito Step 2.

3 The Pepito Step 3.

4 The man ends standing on the right foot, having tapped the left foot across and in front...

5 ...he must now quickly run his left foot around his right foot...

6 ...before continuing back with the left foot into the Doblo Ocho.

4 The Pepito Step 4.

5 On Step 5 of the Pepito, the man will be forward on his left foot, and the woman back on her right.

6 The man leads the Parada and curves his right foot forward into contact with the floor to "stop" the woman as the inside of the ball of his right foot touches the outside of the ball of her left foot. The count is "slow."

COMBINATION THREE – *El Retroceso – Modified Salida – El Ocho Abierto to Parada – La Llevada – El Sandwich continuing with El Ocho and La Resolucion*

This combination starts with the Retroceso and the Modified Salida as described in Group Three. Then a linking piece is introduced which joins the Ocho Abierto with the Parada of Group Seven.

1 Dance the five counts of the Retroceso...

3 For the linking piece, the man leads the woman to dance by his side. The woman walks forward with the right foot between herself and the man's side. (Count – quick)

2 ...and the Modified Salida.

4 The man keeps the right foot in place, and swivels a quarter turn to the right. The woman steps to the side with the left foot making a quarter turn to the right to face the man.

5 The man swivels a quarter turn to the right, extends the right leg, with knees together. His arms are extended to guide the woman back into a Parada.

▶ **6** Continue with the Llevada...

▼ **7**...the Sandwich...

8 ...and the Ocho, finishing with the Resolucion.

COMBINATION FOUR – *La Media Luna – La Parada*

Here is another example of how one figure can be made to join with another without interrupting the flow of movement. In this combination, because the man will not be closing the feet on Step 7, the left knee remains flexed. Dance up to Step 6 of the Media Luna. Dance the Parada, then continue with the Sandwich or the Llevada.

Left: For the Parada, curve the right foot forward in contact with the floor, so that the ball of the foot makes contact with the outside of the ball of the woman's left foot.

El Gancho (The Hook)

The Gancho is one of the most famous embellishments in Tango and can make even basic figures impressive. The move itself is a type of hooking kick performed below the partner's leg. Because a Gancho is an extra embellishment to the move being danced, it has to be fast. It is therefore danced on an "and" count inserted into the normal timing.

You will now discover the intricacies of performing a Gancho, but take care to follow the guide exactly or there may be an injury! A Gancho can be danced following the Sandwich in any of the groups or combinations containing that figure.

Start where the man has danced the Sandwich and has ended on his right foot, with knees together, right knee flexed and the left leg extending straight forward. The woman has transferred her weight forward and is standing on the left foot.

1 Man

Lead the woman to step forward across you, not too close but rotating slightly clockwise. (Count – slow)

Woman

Walk forward onto the right foot over the man's left foot. (Count – slow)

2 Man

Check the woman across the waist with your right arm and lead her to step backwards by rotating anticlockwise. At the same time, leaving the ball of the left foot on the floor, lift the left knee, ensuring that your knees are now spread open (Count – slow)

Woman

Lift the left foot back over the man's left foot, transfer your weight back onto it and relax the left knee. You should now feel the man's left knee beneath you. (Count – slow) If you do not feel the man's knee, do not Gancho!

3 Man

Hold the position while the woman performs the Gancho. (Count – &)

Woman

Ensuring that your knees are together, curve the right foot backwards beneath the man's thigh in the hooking kick of the Gancho. (Count – &)

Style Tip

During the Gancho, the man's weight must remain entirely on the right foot. There is a tendency for men to transfer their weight forward onto the left foot in Step 2. Avoid this or you run the risk of serious injury.

Now continue into the Ocho following a Sandwich.

LA QUEBRADA (THE BREAK)

Right: The Quebrada is not a figure in itself but an action. Meaning a "break", it occurs when one dancer moves their foot to "break" the line between their partner's feet. Normally, though not exclusively, it is the man who performs the Quebrada, which is often the opening for a Sacada or Desplazamiento.

LA SACADA OR EL DESPLAZAMIENTO (THE DISPLACEMENT)

Left: A Sacada or Desplazamiento is a displacement of a partner's foot or leg using one's own foot or leg. When combined with the correct use of the transfer of body weight, this is one of the most powerful leads available to the man, leaving the woman with no option but to comply.

The Final Combination

The Media Luna, a slow, purposeful opening figure, gives the dancers time to establish a rapport and starts to steadily build up the atmosphere and suspense in readiness for the drama which is now about to be played between the dancers. Continue with the Double Start but pause thoughtfully for the Shoeshine while preparing for what follows. The man completes the Shoeshine with an Amague – a frappé with the right foot on an "and" count.

1 – 2 Man
Dance Steps 1 and 2 of the Modified Salida. (Count – quick, quick)

1 Woman
Dance a Modified Salida, as follows. The movement on the "and" count will be assisted by lowering into the left knee at the beginning of the movement. Walk back with the left foot. (Counts – quick, quick)

2 Woman
Walk backwards with the right foot along the same line but turning to maintain parallel shoulders with the man. (Count – quick)

3 Man
Dance the "and" count of the Americano by remaining on the left foot and ensuring that the knees are tightly together. Lift the right foot so that the lower leg is parallel with the floor. Then flick the right foot towards the right. (Count – &)
Woman
Walk forward with the left foot crossing past the right foot and dancing across the man. Swivel on the left foot, turning to the left and preparing to cut across the man's line at 90° to the man, who will be on your right. (Count – &)

QUEBRADAS AND SACADAS

4 Man

As we move into this section, the woman should be in front of you but at 90° to you. As the woman steps forward, place your right foot between her feet – the Quebrada. This move will be assisted by keeping your body weight back at the beginning of the move. Now transfer your weight forward onto the right foot and swivel to the right until your shoulders are parallel with the woman's.
(Count – slow)

Woman

Walk forward onto the right foot at 90° to the man, leaving the left foot in place behind you. (Count – slow)

▶ 5 Man

Bring the left foot forward, brushing past your right foot, and placing it well forward through the woman's legs. Again, hold back the body at the beginning of this step. The outside of your thigh should be in contact with the inside of the woman's thigh as you move your body weight forward – the Sacada. This forces the woman to rotate and step back into a Parada. (Count – slow)

Woman

Swivel on the right foot, turning to the right and stepping to the side onto your left foot to end with your shoulders parallel to the man's. (Count – slow)

6 Man

Swivelling slightly to the right on the left foot, slide the right foot forward in a curving line, keeping your weight on the left foot. With the inside edge of the ball of the right foot, make contact with the outside edge of the ball of the woman's left foot. (Count – slow)

Woman

As you feel the man's Sacada, release the right foot. Swivel to the right on the left foot and, brushing the right foot past the left, step backwards onto the right foot in a Parada. (Count – slow)

▼ **7– 8**

Now continue with a
Llevada or two...
(Counts – &, slow)

▼ **11**

Slip in a surprise
Gancho.
(Count – slow)

▲ **9–10**

... followed by the
Sandwich. (Counts –
slow, slow)

▶ **12** Conclude the Gancho.
(Count – slow)

13–15 Then finish with the Resolucion.
(Counts – quick, quick, slow)

MUSIC SUGGESTION

As you become more interested and experienced at dancing Tango, do remember to only dance to authentic "Argentine Tango" music. The best orchestras to look out for include José Basso, Francisco Canaro, Sexteto Mayor, Florinda Sassone, Francisco Lomuto, Hector Varela, Juan d'Arienzo, Armando Pontier, Osvaldo Fresedo, Fulvia Salamanca and the Orchesta Tango Café. Music by Astor Piazzolla, Nestor Marconi and other modern artists are more appropriate for listening to than for dancing.

We hope that you have enjoyed learning some of the basic movements and concepts of authentic Tango Argentino. If you would like to progress further, why not look up the details of your local Tango club? The pleasure is greatly enhanced when it is shared. We wish you many hours of pleasure dancing Tango Argentino!

Further Information

Further information about Tango Argentino dance courses
is available from:

Paul and Elaine Bottomer, 6 Dove Grove, Egginton,
Derbyshire, DE65 6HH, England

Ausdance (National Secretariat), PO Box 45 Braddon
ACT 2601, Australia

Ausdance NSW, Pier 4, The Wharf, Hickson Road, Walsh Bay
NSW 2000, Australia

Ausdance Victoria, 170 Southbank Boulevard, South
Melbourne, Vic 3205, Australia

Café Tango 4848 Boulevard Saint-Laurent, Montreal,
Quebec, Canada

Tango Libre, 1650 Marie-Anne Est, Montreal,
Quebec, Canada

Acknowledgements
The author and publishers would like to thank the following for their participation in the photography of
this book. Their dance skills and enthusiasm were invaluable:
Elaine Bottomer, Trevor and Naomi Ironmonger, Tanya Janes, Philippe Laue and Mina di Placido

We gratefully acknowledge the kind permission of Sounds Sensational to use references from *Tango
Argentino: The Technique* by Paul Bottomer and for their co-operation in the preparation of this
publication.

Tango Argentino: The Technique (book)
Tango Argentino (instructional video – PAL/NTSC/SECAM)
Orchestra Tango Café Plays Tango Argentino (CD, MC, LP)
All available from Sounds Sensational, 38 Katherine Drive, Toton, Nottingham NG9 6JB, England

Picture Credits
The publishers would like to thank Trip/D. Saunders for permission to reproduce the photograph on
page 8.